Shaun's Lawn

by Lauren Quillin
illustrated by Susan Lexa

Practice Decodable 77

McGraw Hill Education

Bothell, WA • Chicago, IL • Columbus, OH • New York, NY

MHEonline.com

Send all inquiries to:
McGraw-Hill Education
8787 Orion Place
Columbus, OH 43240

ISBN: 978-0-02-144785-5
MHID: 0-02-144785-3

Printed in China.

8 9 10 11 12 DSS 27 26 25 24 23

Shaun planted a new lawn. It took a long time. Tired Shaun yawned as he turned the faucet.

Later, cawing sounds woke Shaun up.
"Crows are eating my lawn!"
Shaun ran out and yelled, "Scram!"

The crows did scram at first. Then Shaun looked out. He saw crows! Shaun needed a plan.

Shaun stuffed a shirt and pants with straw. Did that help? No! Shaun saw crows pecking the straw!

Shaun stuck a plastic owl on an awning.
Crows hate owls. Yet this owl did not fool crows.

Shaun played sounds of squawking hawks.
Hawks frighten crows. The crows left at last!